THE
GOOF-PROOFER

Stephen Johnson Manhard

D1053642

COLLIER BOOKS
Macmillan Publishing Company
New York
Collier Macmillan Publishers
London

Copyright © 1985, 1987 by Stephen J. Manhard

All rights reserved.
No part of this book may be reproduced or transmitted in any
form or by any means, electronic or mechanical, including photo-
copying, recording, or by any information storage and retrieval
system, without permission in writing from the Publisher.

MACMILLAN PUBLISHING COMPANY
866 Third Avenue, New York, N.Y. 10022
Collier Macmillan Canada, Inc.

Library of Congress Cataloging-in-Publication Data

Manhard, Stephen Johnson.
The goof-proofer.

1. English language—Usage. 2. English language—
Grammar—1950–   . I. Title.
PE112.M29   1987   428   87-6317

ISBN: 0-02-040610-X

Macmillan books are available at special discounts for bulk
purchases for sales promotions, premiums, fund-raising, or edu-
cational use. For details, contact:

Special Sales Director
Macmillan Publishing Company
866 Third Avenue
New York, N.Y. 10022

10 9 8 7

PRINTED IN THE UNITED STATES OF AMERICA

Contents

Contents

Contents

Preface

My aim in writing *The Goof-Proofer* is twofold:

1) To provide an easy-to-use, uncomplicated learning tool for those who have been deprived of good grounding in the proper usage of the English language;

2) To provide a convenient resource to help people in all walks of life—but particularly those involved in communications of any kind—avoid the most common errors in English. I believe that communicators have a special obligation to use the language correctly, because what they say or write has such far-reaching influence for good or ill.

In no way is this book intended to take the place of a grammar textbook. To keep it short and not intimidating, tedious grammatical rules have purposely been omitted and explanations of usages have been simplified. For those who require in-depth study of the intricacies of English, plenty of grammar textbooks are available in bookstores and libraries.

Many people do not have the time or inclination for such study, however, although they recognize the importance of avoiding as many errors as possible. It is my hope that *The Goof-Proofer* will be of help to them—and thus to the preservation of generally accepted standard American English.

S. J. M.

Introduction

Do you realize that English—particularly American English—has become the universally accepted language of international communication throughout the world?

As world trade and multinational companies have proliferated, English has become the indispensable means by which business and professional people throughout our "global village" communicate with one another. A thorough command of standard English has become recognized as essential to success in almost every field of endeavor, no matter what your native tongue.

Eighty percent of the world's computer data is in English. More than half of the world's newspapers are published in English, and the language dominates the airwaves. When a Russian pilot lands a Russian airliner at a Russian airport, he receives instructions in English—because it is the universal language of air-traffic control.

So today, outside the English-speaking nations, the number one foreign language taught in practically every country on earth is English. Two hundred and fifty million Chinese people (more than the entire population of the United States) are now learning English, and it is an embarrassing fact that foreigners often speak and write English more properly than those who have grown up with it.

Because American English is now more widely used than any other language in the history of the world, its *proper* usage is more important to everyone everywhere than ever before.

Whether or not it is your native tongue, people now judge you by the way you speak and write English. The ability—or lack of it—to express yourself clearly and correctly is a yardstick by which others measure your intelligence and level of education.

Learning to use English properly helps students to achieve better grades. It helps business and professional people to obtain better jobs and faster promotions, because good communication skills are critically important in today's complex society. In short, using good English makes a favorable impression and helps you get ahead; using poor English makes a bad impression and holds you back.

It is an unfortunate fact that millions of otherwise well-educated people, even those whose native language is English, are misusing it and making themselves look bad. Why? Because, I think, they have been shortchanged by "permissive" education, which has put more emphasis on self-expression than on the basic rules of English. Too many teachers have graded compositions on content, not grammar or spelling. A whole generation, including many people who are now teaching our children, has been largely deprived of proper grounding in this vital subject.

So now many people, through no fault of their own, are not proficient in the proper use of English, including, alas, far too many professional communicators whose output is read and heard every day.

These constant mistakes in print and on the air are being picked up and repeated by millions of persons who assume that what they read and hear is correct. As these goofs become common usage, our language is continually being undermined. As W. H. Auden, the American poet and teacher, said, "If language is corrupted, thought is corrupted." Unless we clean up our act soon, our ability to communicate clearly and our very culture are in serious jeopardy.

But learning all the complex rules of grammar, spelling, syntax, and punctuation is no picnic when we're young, and it's even tougher when we're older. *The Goof-Proofer* has a different purpose. This innovative little book is designed to help you eliminate the most common and flagrant goofs in your speaking and writing, which make a poor impression, blemish your work, and may be holding you back.

Because I am a retired advertising executive and copywriter, I have written *The Goof-Proofer* from the viewpoint of a communicator, not a teacher. It's not intended to be exhaustive; rather, it simply lists the most common errors, shows you what is *wrong* and what is *right*, and explains how to remember to avoid such goofs.

Whenever you need to refresh your memory, you will find that the compact format of *The Goof-Proofer* makes it a valuable tool to keep at hand for reference anytime.

P.S. As an advertising man, it pains me to admit that advertisers—even the large, national agencies, which formerly maintained high standards—are now among the most flagrant polluters of our language. For example, the famous slogan of some years ago "Winston tastes good *like* a cigarette should" was undoubtedly largely responsible for the now widespread misuse of *like* in place of *as*. As E. B. White has so correctly pointed out in *The Elements of Style*, "Today, the language of advertising enjoys an enormous circulation. With its deliberate infractions of grammatical rules and its crossbreeding of the parts of speech, it profoundly influences the tongues and pens of children and adults. . . . It is the language of mutilation."

The Goof-Proofer is, at least to some extent, an effort to atone for the sins of my profession.

October 1986   Stephen Johnson Manhard
                                                  Foster City, California

Acknowledgment

The author is most grateful to Mary Louise Gilman and the National Shorthand Reporters Association for their kind permission to excerpt portions of her book, *3000 Sound-Alikes and Look-Alikes,* copyright 1982 by the National Shorthand Reporters Association. It is highly recommended to all who feel the need for the most complete compilation and explanation of confusing words available.

The Goof-Proofer is dedicated to my mother, Mary Ida Johnson Manhard, who instilled in me a lifelong love of well-chosen words.

I. How Good Is Your Grasp of English?

To help you find out, here's a little test that's fun to take and may prove quite revealing. This imaginary wire-service story contains numerous errors frequently found in print and broadcast media. As you read the text, mark each goof you spot.

WASHINGTON, D.C.—The steps of the nations capital were the sight of an unusual ceremony today as Secretary of State Horatio Smith addressed the imminent new members of the diplomatic core.

"Its' a pleasure for Jane and myself to welcome you," said Smith, as his wife stood discretely in the background with a navel aid. Dressed in a smart blue surge suit and wearing less jewels than usual, Mrs. Smith looked like she was enjoying the acclimation of the group. Despite the vary cold whether, which didn't seam to phase them, the dignitaries gave free reign to their applause.

Between thirty to forty diplomats listened with rapped attention, standing stationery like gripped in a vice, under the watchful eyes of the Secret Service men their to guard against incidence.

Hardly never at a loss for words, but looking a bit pail, Smith said he hoped his listeners had become use to the bitter cold, the worse the city has scene in years. "Between you and I," he said, "its become so chilly anymore that I'd try and lay in bed on days like this if it were'nt against my principals. Besides, Jane makes me get up early every morning and test my metal by peddling my exorcise bike."

In a more serious vain, the Secretary then told the tail of a racetrack better who lost all his money and, out of shear hunger, had committed a miner theft. He stole an orange, which he was pealing when arrested. On advise of council the gamboler waved a jury trial and through himself on the mercy of the court. As the culprit stood ringing his hands, the judge hit the sealing: He denied bale, meeted out thirty days in jail, and leveed a fine of one hundred dollars.

"The man took his punishment pretty good," said

Smith, "but it was a hard way to learn a lessen we all can prophet from: As we sew, so shall we reap, weather we are individuals or nation's. Let us not reek vengeance on one another. Instead, let us saver the blessings of piece!"

As the teaming crowd began to disburse, the Secretary spied a pare of newlyweds who's bridle party was standing further back in the crowd. A reporter, pouring over his notes, then overheard Smith tell his wife, to who he was whispering, "Like I always say, its alot easier to tie the not than to undue it. I hope they never loose site of that and play it strait. Otherwise, there happiness will just be an allusion and ware off soon. Now I'd like some hot bullion—I feel like I've caught a sleight cold."

Of course you spotted quite a few obvious goofs, but did you catch *all* of them? Check the list on pages 83 and 84, and you may be quite surprised. If you found them all, congratulations! You probably don't need this book. Please pass it on to someone who really does.

II. How *The Goof-Proofer* Works for You

None of us (let's hope!) commits all of the goofs listed herein, but it's a good bet that all of us commit some of them occasionally or even regularly. No matter how good our intentions, we're all prone to forgetfulness and human error.

As you leaf through the following pages, please note that each goof is numbered and accompanied by two boxes labeled GOOF and PROOF. These are designed to help you check and double-check yourself.

For example, if Goof #1 is one that you're sure you never make, check the PROOF box, indicating that you're already "proof" against this goof. But if it's an error that you realize (or perhaps others point out) you do tend to commit, then check the GOOF box, indicating that you need to work on this one. When you've learned how to correct it and are sure that you will avoid it in the future, go back and check the PROOF box, indicating that now you are "proof" against this goof—check and double-check!

The best way to use this book is to first read each goof, think carefully about it, and then check the appropriate GOOF or PROOF box, as outlined above. Then you'll know exactly what you need to work on.

It's Easy to Learn by Example

You'll also see that each goof is illustrated by one or more examples of both the incorrect and the correct usage, headed WRONG and <u>RIGHT</u>. This makes it

4

easy to goof-proof yourself. There are no complicated rules to remember—just what is wrong and what is right. Still, you may not find it all that easy to reprogram yourself and unlearn bad habits accumulated over a period of years. So I suggest that you—

Concentrate on Eliminating
Just *One* Goof per Day

If you can goof-proof yourself considerably faster than that, go for it! But it's a lot better to do a slow and thorough job than a fast, hit-or-miss one. By concentrating on eliminating just one goof per day—memorizing what's wrong and what's right and repeating it often to yourself—you'll soon have every **PROOF** box checked. Your writing and speech will be free of all these common mistakes, and your image as a literate person will be greatly enhanced. You'll also have the satisfaction of knowing that you are doing your part to preserve clear communication and our unifying English language.

III. The Most Common Grammatical Goofs

Misuse of **I**, **Me**, and Other
Personal Pronouns

A) Always use **I** when it's one of the *subjects* of a sentence:

> WRONG: **Me** and Tom laughed.
> RIGHT: Tom and **I** laughed. (Please be polite
> and mention yourself last.)

B) Always use **me** when it's one of the *objects* of a verb or preposition:

> WRONG: She invited Jennifer and **I**.
> RIGHT: She invited Jennifer and **me**.
> (**Me** is the object of the verb *invited*.)

> WRONG: Just between you and **I**, it's true.
> RIGHT: Just between you and **me**, it's true.
> (**Me** is the object of the preposition *between*.)

You wouldn't say "Me laughed" or "She invited I," would you? You already know what's right when there's only one subject or object involved.

Remember that the grammar doesn't change when other subjects or objects are added, and you'll never make these mistakes again!

C) All the other personal pronouns work the same way. Always use **he, she, we,** and **they** when they're one of the *subjects* of a sentence:

> WRONG: **Him (her, us, them)** and you should go.
>
> <u>RIGHT</u>: You and **he (she, we, they)** should go.

D) Always use **him, her, us,** and **them** when they're one of the *objects* of a verb or preposition:

> WRONG: That will help Bill and **he (she, we, they).**
>
> <u>RIGHT</u>: That will help Bill and **him (her, us, them).**
> (**Him, her, us,** and **them** are objects of the verb *help.*)

> WRONG: Joe sent it to Jan and **he (she, we, they)** yesterday.
>
> <u>RIGHT</u>: Joe sent it to Jan and **him (her, us, them)** yesterday.
> (**Him, her, us,** and **them** are objects of the preposition *to.*)

If in doubt, just mentally eliminate the "— and" before the pronoun, and you'll know immediately what's right. Remember, the grammar doesn't change when other subjects or objects are added.

Misuse of the Pronoun **Myself**

Never, *never* (please!) use **myself** as a substitute for **I** or **me.** It's becoming an epidemic!

This glaring goof may be so widespread today because so many people aren't sure whether to use **I** or **me** (as explained in Goof #1), so they cop out by misusing **myself.**

A prominent radio talk-show host (with a Ph.D.!) was just one of countless communicators guilty of this poisoning of our language:

> WRONG: **Myself** and my guest will be right back.
>
> <u>RIGHT</u>: My guest and **I** will be right back. (Always mention yourself last.)

> WRONG: She told Terry and **myself.**
>
> <u>RIGHT</u>: She told Terry and **me.**

The pronoun myself *should be used only reflexively (I hurt* myself*) or for emphasis (I told her* myself*). Using it in place of* I *or* me *is one of the surest ways to draw attention to carelessness or lack of education.*

 **GOOF #3**

Misuse of the Preposition **Like**

Use **like** only before nouns and pronouns, and before gerunds (a verbal form that functions as a noun). Here are two examples:

> <u>RIGHT</u>: He looks **like** his brother and walks **like** him.
> <u>RIGHT</u>: I don't feel **like** eating or drinking.

Never use **like** before phrases and clauses, where **as, as if, as though,** or **that** is proper. Try to remember not to commit these types of flagrant errors, which are heard constantly on the air and are seen far too frequently in print:

> WRONG: **Like** I said before, it's true.
> <u>RIGHT</u>: **As** I said before, it's true.

> WRONG: He looks **like** he's happy.
> <u>RIGHT</u>: He looks **as if (as though)** he's happy.

> WRONG: I feel **like** I should go.
> <u>RIGHT</u>: I feel **that** I should go.

As an adman, I deplore that infamous slogan "Winston tastes good like *a cigarette should," which popularized the misuse of* like *in place of* as!

GOOF #4

Misuse of the Apostrophe (')

This is the most common error in print. The apostrophe has only *two* proper uses:*

1) To indicate possession;
2) To indicate the omission of one or more letters.

Use #1, indicating possession:

   WRONG: She saw the **mans** face.
   <u>RIGHT</u>: She saw the **man's** face.

Caution: Never put an apostrophe in these pronouns that are *already* possessive: **its, his, hers, theirs, yours, ours,** and **whose.** See related Goofs #5 and #6, which follow.

Use #2, indicating omission of letter(s):

   WRONG: **Your** looking very nice today.
   <u>RIGHT</u>: **You're** (you are) looking very nice today.

Caution: Never put an apostrophe before the "s" in a word you just want to make plural:*

   WRONG: I read two **book's** last month.
   <u>RIGHT</u>: I read two **books** last month.

---

* *Exception:* The apostrophe is used when writing plural letters (watch your p's and q's) or plural years (the 1980's).

When you want to make a word **plural** AND **possessive**, be sure to put an apostrophe *after* the "s":

    WRONG: He liked the **girls** appearance.

    WRONG: He liked the **girl's** appearance. (*This refers to only one girl.*)

    <u>RIGHT</u>: He liked the **girls'** appearance. (*This refers to more than one girl.*)

GOOF #5

Misuse of **Its** and **It's**

As small as they are, these two little words account for some of the most flagrant misuses of the apostrophe and confusion of meaning (see also Goof #6).

Its is a possessive pronoun and does not need an apostrophe to make it indicate possession:

WRONG: The dog wagged **it's** tail.
<u>RIGHT</u>: The dog wagged **its** tail.

When you put an apostrophe in the word and make it **it's,** you change the meaning entirely. Now you have indicated the omission of a letter (*i*), turning the word into the contraction of **it is:**

WRONG: **Its** a very bushy tail.
<u>RIGHT</u>: **It's** (it is) a very bushy tail.

WRONG: The dog thinks **its** fun to chase **it's** tail.
<u>RIGHT</u>: The dog thinks **it's** fun to chase **its** tail.

If you'll just give it a little thought, it's *not too hard to put the apostrophe in* its *rightful place and make sure of* its *absence where* it's *out of place.*

 **GOOF #6**

Misuse of **Whose** and **Who's**

Here's another case where the use of the apostrophe—
or the lack of it—continually causes confusion of two
words that sound alike but have entirely different
meanings.

Whose is a possessive pronoun that you should
never mess up with an apostrophe:

WRONG: **Who's** (or **who'se**) bat is this?
  RIGHT: **Whose** bat is this?

Who's is the contraction of **who is;** the apostrophe
does not indicate possession but the omission of the
letter "i":

WRONG: **Whose** on first, using **who's** glove?
  RIGHT: **Who's** (who is) on first, using **whose**
        glove?

Who's *the communicator* whose *understanding of
proper English usage is rapidly improving? I hope it's
you, dear reader!*

GOOF #7

Misuse of Verbs That Don't Agree in Number with Their Subjects

If the subject is singular, its verb must also be singular; if the subject is plural, its verb must also be plural, of course. It's all too easy to violate this important rule and look dumb, because there are confusing pitfalls.

One pitfall occurs when modifying words that are plural come between a singular subject and its verb:

> WRONG: His list of honors and qualifications **are** impressive.
> RIGHT: His list of honors and qualifications **is** impressive.

Remember that *list*, not *honors and qualifications*, is the subject and requires a singular verb.

Another trap to avoid: Distributive words such as **none, either, neither, everybody, nobody,** and **each** are often thought of as plural but are actually singular and take singular verbs:

> WRONG: None of us **have** enough money.
> RIGHT: None of us **has** enough money.

> WRONG: Neither of you **are** right.
> RIGHT: Neither of you **is** right.

> WRONG: Each of the three women **were** attractive.

<u>**RIGHT**</u>: Each of the three women **was** attractive.

Misuse of Pronouns That Don't Agree in Number or Case with Their Antecedents

Here again, pitfalls make it easy to mess up, so be on your guard.

One pitfall is collective nouns, such as *committee*. The word is singular but is often thought of as plural because it's made up of several people:

> WRONG: The committee announced **they** would meet.
>
> RIGHT: The committee announced **it** would meet.

Note: An important exception to the agreement rule is now becoming accepted to avoid the following dilemma: In the past, the masculine pronoun has been used to include both male and female, as in "Everyone has **his** choice." But with the rise of feminism this has been construed to be sexist, and the grammatical ways to avoid the problem are awkward: "Everyone has **his** or **her** choice" or "Everyone has **one's** choice." So the grammatically incorrect "Everyone has **their** choice" has come into widespread use.

While purists still decry this, the eminent grammarian Fowler decided that there is no entirely happy solution and that "everyone must decide for **himself,** for **himself and herself,** or for **themselves.**" I'll go along with him, because I recognize that our language

16

inevitably changes as society changes—and this is a perfect example of such change.

Another pitfall to avoid: A pronoun following any form of the verb **to be (am, are, is, was, were)** takes the *nominative*, not *objective*, case—even though it may sound stilted:

> **WRONG:** The person who called was **him.**
> <u>RIGHT</u>: The person who called was **he.**

An easy way to remember what's right is to turn the sentence around: **He** was the person who called. You surely wouldn't say "**Him** was the person"! Note that the pronoun **he** now correctly agrees in case (nominative) with the subject, *person.*

When a pronoun is combined with a modifying noun, it creates another trap that's all too easy to fall into:

> **WRONG:** He took **we** customers to the game.
> <u>RIGHT</u>: He took **us** customers to the game.

If you simply drop the modifying noun, *customers,* from the sentence, the correct form is immediately clear: You wouldn't say "He took **we,**" would you? Note again that the pronoun **us** now correctly agrees in case (objective) with the object, *customers.*

Misuse of Double Comparisons

I saw an automobile ad recently that claimed the car was "more roomier" than its competitors. Fire the copywriter!

Never use **more** or **most** when **-er** or **-est** is added to a modifier:

WRONG: Your car is **more roomier** than mine.
<u>RIGHT</u>: Your car is **roomier** (or **more roomy**) than mine.

WRONG: That's the **most stupidest** thing I ever heard.
<u>RIGHT</u>: That's the **stupidest** (or **most stupid**) thing I ever heard.

Using a double comparison doesn't double the impact of a statement. It's just a singularly flagrant goof!

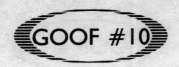 **GOOF #10**

GOOF

PROOF

Misuse of Double Negatives

The use of double negatives is so widely recognized as a prime example of illiteracy that I hesitate even to include it—but it still crops up too often, especially in sportscasting.

Two negatives (such as **no, none, nobody, not, can't, couldn't, wouldn't, shouldn't, never, nothing, hardly,** or **scarcely**) should *never* be used in the same statement:

WRONG: The plays he called **hardly never** seemed to work.

RIGHT: The plays he called **hardly ever** (or **never**) seemed to work.

WRONG: That pitcher **can't** strike out **nobody**.

RIGHT: That pitcher **can't** strike out **anybody** (or) That pitcher **can** strike out **nobody**.

WRONG: I told him he **couldn't** have **none**.

RIGHT: I told him he **couldn't** have **any** (or) I told him he **could** have **none**.

Using a double negative doesn't double the impact of a statement. It just creates a very negative impression of your education level.

19

Misuse of **Between** . . . **To**

How this corruption originated is a mystery to me,
but lately it seems to be cropping up more and more
frequently in both print and broadcast media. Let's
try to nip it in the bud!

Standard usage has always been:

between . . . and (or) **from . . . to.**

You may take your pick; both are correct. But *never*,
please, mix up the two phrases!

WRONG: The plane flew **between** New York **to**
Chicago.

RIGHT: The plane flew **between** New York **and**
Chicago
(or) The plane flew **from** New York **to**
Chicago.

Just between *you* and *me, it's easy to change* from
wrong to *right if you'll just practice a bit.*

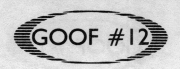

☐ GOOF

☐ PROOF

Misuse of **Anymore** for **Lately, Nowadays,** or **Today**

Nowadays **anymore** is regularly being misused by people who really mean **nowadays** or **today** (at the present time):

WRONG: This word is widely misused **anymore.**
RIGHT: This word is widely misused **lately** (**nowadays** or **today**).

Note: **Anymore** is properly used in statements involving a change in a previous activity or condition:

RIGHT: I don't go there **anymore.**
RIGHT: Why don't you like her **anymore?**

If you're in the habit of saying things such as "Houses are too expensive anymore," *please don't make yourself sound dumb* anymore. *Instead, say* nowadays *or* today *and be right!*

GOOF

PROOF

Misuse of **And** after **Try**

In some cases *American* English differs from *English* English, and this is one of them. We continually hear **try and** in English television shows, but it grates on American ears, except perhaps in the slang expression *try and stop me.*

The verb *try* should be followed by **to,** not **and,** in all careful communication:

WRONG: Please try **and** remember this.
RIGHT: Please try **to** remember this.

Even when it results in **a to** on both sides of *try,* the rule still holds:

WRONG: She ought to try **and** do it.
RIGHT: She ought to try **to** do it.

Try to *bear in mind that* try and *is not standard American English.*

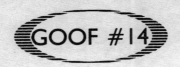 **GOOF #14**

GOOF

PROOF

Misuse of **Hopefully**

Hopefully is a perfectly good word, but lately its misuse has become so widespread that it may already be too late to halt this corruption of our language. **Hopefully** means exactly what it says: **full of hope**. Its correct usage, therefore, is in statements that indicate a person is **hopeful**, such as:

> <u>RIGHT</u>: "Will you help me?" she asked **hopefully.**

It is *not* correct to use the adverb **hopefully** to mean "I hope" or "it is to be hoped":

> <u>WRONG</u>: "**Hopefully**, he'll help me," she said.
> <u>RIGHT</u>: "**I hope** he'll help me," she said.

It's difficult not to let a misuse like this one, which is constantly seen and heard, creep into your vocabulary; I frequently have to correct myself. But I hope that you'll remember not to use hopefully *when you mean* I hope!

Misuse of **Could of** and **Could have**

Recently I've seen this flagrant grammatical goof more and more often in print, apparently because poorly taught writers think they hear **could of** when people shorten **could have** to **could've** in conversation. There is no such phrase as **could of**:

WRONG: I **could of** danced all night.
<u>RIGHT</u>: I **could have** danced all night.

Saying or writing could of *is one of the prime telltale tip-offs that your education in English has been sadly neglected. Being guilty of this goof* could have *been the reason you made a poor impression that is holding you back.*

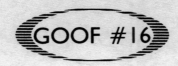

GOOF #16

Misuse of **Different Than**

Here's another very common grammatical gaffe that's heard and seen far too often. It's easy to avoid if you just remember that one thing differs **from** another; surely you wouldn't say that one thing differs **than** another:

> WRONG: She's very different **than** her sister.
> <u>RIGHT</u>: She's very different **from** her sister.

Saying or writing different than *is a sure way to call attention to the fact that you're* different from *those who use our language correctly.*

Misuse of **More** (or **Most**) **Unique**

The dictionary defines **unique** as "being the only one of its kind; without an equal or equivalent." A thing is either unique or it isn't, so there can't be any qualification of degree. Advertisers, I'm sorry to admit, are among the worst offenders; they frequently claim that a product or service is "the **most unique**" on the market:

WRONG: This is the **most unique** computer ever designed.

RIGHT: This computer has **a unique** design (or) This computer is truly **unique**.

WRONG: His watch is **more unique** than mine.
RIGHT: His watch is **more unusual** than mine.

It's not uniquely *wrong to say* more *or* most unique, *because so many others are guilty of it too; it's just plain wrong!*

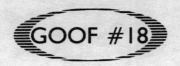 **GOOF #18**

Misuse of **These** (or **Those**) **Kind**

As we've seen previously, pronouns must agree in number with the words to which they refer. If you remember this rule, you'll see why it's incorrect to say or write **these (those) kind**. **These** and **those** are plurals of **this** and **that**, while **kind** is singular; they don't properly agree.

> WRONG: **These (those) kind** of food is fattening.
> <u>RIGHT</u>: **These (those) kinds** of food are fattening.

Of course you can also correct the statement by making the words singular instead of plural:

> <u>RIGHT</u>: **This (that) kind** of food is fattening.

Just be sure to keep both words singular or both words plural. When they're in agreement, you won't be caught making these kinds *of goofs . . . or* this kind *of goof, if you prefer.*

27

Misuse of **Data, Media, Strata, Criteria,** and **Phenomena** with Singular Verbs

It's a singular mistake to treat these words, as so many do, as *singular*. They are the plurals of **datum, medium, stratum, criterion,** and **phenomenon** and should be used with *plural* verbs.

We frequently read and hear errors such as "the **data** *shows* that . . ." and "the **media** *reports* that . . ." and unfortunately these words are rapidly gaining acceptance as singulars:

WRONG: The **data** he showed *was* convincing.
<u>RIGHT</u>: The **data** he showed *were* convincing.

WRONG: The **media** *is* incorrect far too often.
<u>RIGHT</u>: The **media** *are* incorrect far too often.

Remember that radio, for example, is one **medium** of communication. When we refer to more than one medium—lumping together radio, television, newspapers, and so forth—we obviously must use the plural of *medium*, which is **media. Data, strata, criteria,** and **phenomena** all work the same way. Now it's easy to see why these words require plural verbs, isn't it?

If it isn't, just take my word for it: Use plural verbs with these four words, and you'll look singularly smart!

28

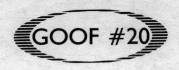 GOOF #20

 GOOF

PROOF

Misuse of **A** and **An**

Can you believe that educated people are now misusing two of the shortest, most common words in the English language? I couldn't until several horrible examples came to my attention, including "**an** judge" (Associated Press), "**a** opportunity" (Writers Guild newsletter), and "**an** professor" (university instructor with a Ph.D. degree)!

The rule is very simple: Use **a** before words beginning with a consonant or consonant sound; use **an** before words beginning with a vowel or vowel sound:

WRONG: Tom gave me **a** apple.
RIGHT: Tom gave me **an** apple.

WRONG: Dottie is **an** skilled typist.
RIGHT: Dottie is **a** skilled typist.

Note: Remember that the vowel **u** often has a consonant sound (*yew*) at the beginning of words such as *union* and *university;* they therefore must be preceded by **a** even though they start with a vowel.

For some reason (perhaps a holdover from England, where initial *h's* are often not pronounced) many people incorrectly use **an** before such words as *hotel, historical,* and *hysterical.* Remember that these words begin with the consonant *h* and must be preceded by **a.** However, when the *h* is silent, as in *herb* or *heir,* **an** is correct.

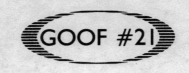

Misuse of **Reknown** for **Renowned**

Lately more and more people commit goofs by writing and saying **reknown** (apparently because of confusion with **known**) when they mean **renowned**.

There are two important points to remember:

1) There is no such word as **reknown**;
2) **Renown** (without a *k*) is a noun that means *fame*; if you want to say a person or thing is *famous*, you must use the corresponding adjective, **renowned**.

> WRONG: Lincoln was a statesman of wide **reknown**.
>
> RIGHT: Lincoln was a statesman of wide **renown**.

> WRONG: Lincoln was a **reknown** statesman.
> RIGHT: Lincoln was a **renowned** statesman.

If you habitually misuse reknown *to mean famous, you'll become* renowned *yourself for committing illiterate goofs.*

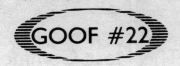 **GOOF #22**

 GOOF

PROOF

Misuse of **For Free**

Here's another prime example of a silly aberration, which has become so accepted that the proper use of the simple adverb **free** is seldom seen or heard these days.

In the sense of without cost, **free** means *for nothing.* When you say **for free,** therefore, you are really saying *for for nothing*—flagrantly redundant double-talk:

> WRONG: Chris got his second cup of coffee **for free.**
>
> RIGHT: Chris got his second cup of coffee **free.**

I know this constantly seen-and-heard goof is easy to commit, because I caught plenty of flak when I was quoted (probably correctly, alas) as saying for free *during a* Wall Street Journal *interview. Moral: If you want to stay* free *of criticism, keep your speech and writing completely* free *of* for free*!*

IV. The Most Commonly Confused Words
(*Arranged in Alphabetical Order*)

GOOF

PROOF

GOOF #23

Confusion of **Affect** and **Effect**

These frequently confused words have similar but definitely different meanings. **Affect** means *to have an influence on* or *cause a change in*. The verb **effect** means *to produce a result* or *bring about*. These examples should make the difference clear:

WRONG: Smoking can adversely **effect** health.
<u>RIGHT</u>: Smoking can adversely **affect** health.

WRONG: Quitting may **affect** an improvement.
<u>RIGHT</u>: Quitting may **effect** an improvement.

Note: To compound the confusion, **effect** is also a *noun,* which is properly used as follows: Smoking can have an adverse **effect** on health.

Learning to use these words correctly can help effect *a favorable change in the way people judge you,* affect *your career, and thus have a good* effect *on your earning power.*

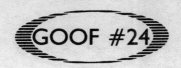 **GOOF #24**

GOOF

PROOF

Confusion of **Aggravate** and **Irritate**

Many people use **aggravate** to mean **irritate**. This may be acceptable as colloquial speech, but the words should not be confused in careful writing. **Aggravate** means *to make worse;* **irritate** means *to exasperate or inflame*. Notice the difference in these examples:

WRONG: His careless writing **aggravated** me.
RIGHT: His careless writing **irritated** me.

WRONG: The bad weather **irritated** my cold.
RIGHT: The bad weather **aggravated** my cold.

Confusing these words may irritate *people and* aggravate *the situation you're in.*

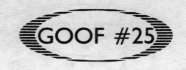
Confusion of **Allude** and **Elude**

These verbs are called *homonyms* or *homophones*—words that sound the same or nearly the same but differ in spelling and meaning. As you might expect, these rascals cause a great deal of confusion, so be on your guard! (You'll find a very handy list of some of the most troublesome homonyms beginning on page 53.)

Allude means *to make an indirect reference to.* **Elude** means *to evade or escape from.* If you use one of these words when you mean the other, the result can be rather ridiculous:

WRONG: Harry **eluded** to his girlfriend.
 RIGHT: Harry **alluded** to his girlfriend.

WRONG: The runner cleverly **alluded** the tackler.
 RIGHT: The runner cleverly **eluded** the tackler.

When you allude *to the right word instead of the wrong one, you* elude *criticism.*

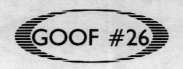

GOOF

PROOF

Confusion of **Bad** and **Badly**

Bad (like **good**) should be used with descriptive verbs such as **look, feel, sound,** and **taste:**

WRONG: Bert's black eye looked very **badly.**
<u>RIGHT</u>: Bert's black eye looked very **bad.**

WRONG: I felt **badly** about being late.
<u>RIGHT</u>: I felt **bad** about being late.

Badly (like **well**) should be used with all other verbs:

WRONG: The team lost because it played **bad.**
<u>RIGHT</u>: The team lost because it played **badly.**

Misusing the language badly *will make you look* bad *and hold you back.*

GOOF

PROOF

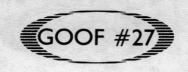

Confusion of **Can** and **May**

"Can we talk?" the woman asks the man. What a silly question! Of course they can talk, unless their tongues are tied, because **can** denotes the *ability* to do something. What she should say is "May we talk?" because **may** denotes *permission* to do something, the meaning she intends.

Remember that when you ask permission, **may** is not only the correct word, it's also the *polite* word:

WRONG: **Can** I read your letter from Joan?
<u>RIGHT</u>: **May** I read your letter from Joan?

This sentence clearly illustrates the difference between the two words:

<u>RIGHT</u>: You **may** read the letter if you **can** find it.

You can *make a better impression by using* may *correctly and politely when asking permission.*

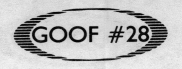

Confusion of **Comprise** and **Compose**

These words confuse so many people that they seem to be misused more often than not. The way to remember the difference is this: The whole **comprises** the parts; the parts **compose** the whole.

These examples should help to make it clearer:

WRONG: The team **composes** eleven players.
<u>RIGHT</u>: The team **comprises** eleven players.

WRONG: Eleven players **comprise** the team.
<u>RIGHT</u>: Eleven players **compose** the team.

WRONG: The team is **comprised** of eleven players.
<u>RIGHT</u>: The team is **composed** of eleven players.

It is confusing, isn't it? Maybe it's simpler and safer to avoid these words entirely and say "The team is made up of eleven players" or "Eleven players make up the team."

Confusion of **Disinterested** and **Uninterested**

Most people think these words are synonymous or interchangeable, but there's an important difference between them. **Disinterested** means *impartial*. **Uninterested** means *indifferent to* or *not interested in*. Notice the distinction in these examples:

WRONG: An umpire should be **uninterested**.
<u>RIGHT</u>: An umpire should be **disinterested**.

WRONG: Ted was **disinterested** in the dull lecture.
<u>RIGHT</u>: Ted was **uninterested** in the dull lecture.

If you're asked to settle a dispute, try to be completely disinterested *even though you may be* uninterested *in being the referee.*

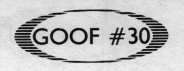

Confusion of **Farther** and **Further**

This has been committed so frequently in the media that millions of people are misusing these words nowadays, but there's an easy way to remember which is which.

When you refer to *physical distance*, always use **farther**—the word that has **far** in it:

WRONG: New York is **further** east than St. Louis.

RIGHT: New York is **farther** east than St. Louis.

Use **further** when you refer to *additional time* or *amount*:

WRONG: This requires **farther** study.

RIGHT: This requires **further** study.

WRONG: Schedule the meeting **farther** in the future.

RIGHT: Schedule the meeting **further** in the future.

The farther *you travel on your vacation, the* further *your bank account will drop.*

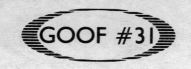
Confusion of **Fewer** and **Less**

Here's a very simple rule to help you be **less** confused about the distinction between these words and make **fewer** misuses of them.

Fewer refers to things that *can* be counted:

> WRONG: **Less** people voted this year.
> RIGHT: **Fewer** people voted this year.

Less refers to things that *cannot* be counted:

> WRONG: He has **fewer** brains than she does.
> RIGHT: He has **less** brains than she does.

Exception: In some cases, when referring to time or money, **less** is correct:

> RIGHT: It took Jean **less** than five minutes to spend a little **less** than one hundred dollars.

However, you would say "I have **fewer** hours of spare time than Sam does" and "I have **fewer** dollars to spend than Sue does." It does get confusing, doesn't it?

GOOF #32

GOOF

PROOF

Confusion of **Fortunate** and **Fortuitous**

Contrary to popular opinion, these words are *not* synonymous. Many people say **fortuitous** (*happening by chance*) when they mean **fortunate** (*lucky or auspicious*). It is okay to say that an encounter was **fortuitous** if it was both lucky and accidental, but if it was only lucky, you should say **fortunate**:

> WRONG: My appointment with Bill proved to be **fortuitous**.
>
> RIGHT: My appointment with Bill proved to be **fortunate**.

If an encounter was merely accidental, you should say **fortuitous**:

> RIGHT: Running across Sue at the supermarket was **fortuitous**; I had been hoping to see her.

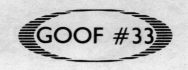

GOOF #33

Confusion of **Good** and **Well**

This very common error seems to occur most often in sports broadcasts and on the sports pages. Could it be because many student athletes seem to spend more time practicing for games than learning to speak proper English?

Good should be used with descriptive verbs such as **look, feel, sound,** and **taste:**

WRONG: This beer tastes **well.**
RIGHT: This beer tastes **good.**

WRONG: The quarterback is looking **well** today.*
RIGHT: The quarterback is looking **good** today.

Remember to use **well** with all other verbs:

WRONG: The team is playing **good** today.
RIGHT: The team is playing **well** today.

Use well *to refer to one's* state of health; *use* good *to refer to one's* appearance.

---

* *This is correct, however, if you mean he looks* healthy.

Confusion of **Imply** and **Infer**

It's amazing how many "well-educated" people get these two little words mixed up or think they are synonymous. They aren't. **Imply** means to *state indirectly;* **infer** means to *draw a conclusion.* Notice the important difference:

WRONG: From the size of his car, she **implied** that he was rich.

RIGHT: From the size of his car, she **inferred** that he was rich.

WRONG: Al meant to **infer** that Steve was misinformed, not lying.

RIGHT: Al meant to **imply** that Steve was misinformed, not lying.

When a friend implies *that you misused a word, you should* infer *that he's trying to be helpful, not critical.*

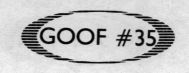

Confusion of **Lay** and **Lie**

If we're not careful, even the best of us mess this up rather regularly. Here's an easy way to remember which to use.

Lay means *to place something down* and *takes an object* (a transitive verb):

> WRONG: **Lie** your head on the pillow.
> <u>RIGHT</u>: **Lay** your head on the pillow.

Lie means *to recline or be situated* and *does not take an object* (an intransitive verb):

> WRONG: **Lay** down on the bed.
> <u>RIGHT</u>: **Lie** down on the bed.

This sentence should make the distinction quite clear:

> <u>RIGHT</u>: **Lie** down on the bed and **lay** your head
> on the pillow.

Adding to the confusion is the fact that the past tense of **lie** is **lay,** and the past tense of **lay** is **laid**—as correctly used in the following example:

> <u>RIGHT</u>: He **lay** down on the sofa after he **laid**
> the book on the table.

English can be tough, and that's no lie!

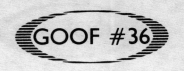

Confusion of **Lend** and **Loan**

Although many people use these words interchangeably as verbs, careful speakers and writers observe the distinction that **lend** is the correct *verb*, while **loan** is a *noun* meaning *money or something else lent for temporary use* and should not be used as a verb:

> WRONG: Joe asked Jim to **loan** him ten dollars.
> RIGHT: Joe asked Jim to **lend** him ten dollars.

> WRONG: Please **loan** me your lawn mower.
> RIGHT: Please **lend** me your lawn mower.

The proper usage of the two words is clearly illustrated in this example:

> RIGHT: If she asks for the **loan** of my car, I'll be glad to **lend** it to her.

They say distance lends *enchantment, but not when the distant person hasn't repaid the* loan *he received from you.*

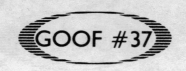

Confusion of **That** and **Which**

Here's another case where many people use the words interchangeably, but you shouldn't if you want to be absolutely correct.

That is properly used to introduce a restrictive, or defining, clause (which *identifies* what is being talked about) and is not preceded by a comma:

> WRONG: Gwen liked the book **which** I gave her.
> RIGHT: Gwen liked the book **that** I gave her.

Which should be used to introduce a nonrestrictive, or nondefining, clause (which gives *additional information* about the subject that has already been identified) and is always preceded by a comma:

> WRONG: The book I gave Gwen, **that** she liked, was written by Mark Twain.
> RIGHT: The book I gave Gwen, **which** she liked, was written by Mark Twain.

Note: In some cases it is permissible to use **which** to introduce a restrictive clause to avoid repetition of the word **that** in a preceding phrase:

> RIGHT: I gave Gwen **that** book **which** I thought she would like.

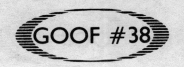 **GOOF #38**

□ GOOF

□ PROOF

Confusion of **Use** and **Used to**

The verb **use** is correctly employed in the past tense with **to** (**used to**) to indicate a former state or regular practice. But today we frequently see and hear the aberration **use to**—probably because that's the way it sounds when **used to** is not carefully enunciated.

This goof will make you look very careless, so be sure to avoid it, especially in writing:

WRONG: We **use to** go there all the time.
<u>RIGHT</u>: We **used to** go there all the time.

WRONG: Betty couldn't get **use to** the heat.
<u>RIGHT</u>: Betty couldn't get **used to** the heat.

When you become used to *avoiding goofs like* use to, *you'll make a much better impression.*

Confusion of **Who** and **That**

The countless communicators **who** stumble over this one will probably never appear in *Who's Who!*

Always use **who** to refer to *persons:*

WRONG: The man **that** won was very happy.
<u>RIGHT</u>: The man **who** won was very happy.

Exception: **That** is correct when referring to a class, species, or type of person: *They are the kind of students that does well in English.*

Use **that** to refer only to *animals* and *things:*

WRONG: This is the dog **who** barked.
<u>RIGHT</u>: This is the dog **that** barked.

WRONG: Alice misses the tree **who** died.
<u>RIGHT</u>: Alice misses the tree **that** died.

People who *learn to use words* that *are correct usually get ahead of those* who *don't.*

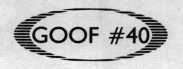

Confusion of **Who** and **Whom**

This is another one that is confused by multitudes of people **who** forget "for **whom** the bell tolls."

Who always refers to the *subject* of the statement. **Whom** always refers to the *object* of the statement. That's not too hard to remember, but confusion arises because people often mix up the subject and object, especially when the sentence is a little involved:

WRONG: Joe asked **whom** was coming to see us.
<u>RIGHT</u>: Joe asked **who** was coming to see us.

Note that **who** is correct because it's the subject of *was coming*, not the object of *asked*.

WRONG: The man **who** Jan preferred was handsome.
<u>RIGHT</u>: The man **whom** Jan preferred was
handsome.

Note that **whom** is correct because it refers to the object of *preferred*, not the subject of *was*.

If you're a person who *can't distinguish between the subject and the object, ask not for* whom *the bell tolls. It tolls for thee!*

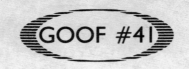

GOOF #41

Confusion of **Worse** and **Worst**

For some reason, more and more people seem to be using **worse** when they mean **worst**. It's a flagrant goof that signals a sad gap in their education, so remember to be careful in statements such as these:

WRONG: It was the **worse** mistake he ever made.
RIGHT: It was the **worst** mistake he ever made.

WRONG: If **worse** comes to **worse**, I'll give in.
RIGHT: If **worst** comes to **worst**, I'll give in.*

Worst (not **worse**!) is also the word you want in the idioms **at worst, get the worst of it,** and **in the worst way.**

It's bad *to misuse words in speech; it's* worse *to misuse them in writing; it's* worst *of all not to care about goofs!*

---

* Some dictionaries list "if *worse* comes to *worst*" as an alternate version of this idiom; take your choice.

V. Nonexistent Words That Are Frequently Misused

How, you may well ask, can people misuse words that do not exist? I can't explain how or why these aberrations have come into common use, but the fact is that countless speakers and writers misuse them every day.

If you are guilty of any of these glaring goofs, try hard to remember that "there ain't no such" words—because misusing them immediately brands you as a person whose English education has been sadly neglected.

WRONG:	RIGHT:
Alot	A lot
Alright	All right
Analyzation	Analysis
Heighth	Height
Interpretate	Interpret
Irregardless	Regardless
Marshall	Marshal
Momento	Memento
Renumeration	Remuneration
Restauranteur	Restaurateur
Smoothe	Smooth
Unequivocably	Unequivocally

VI. Words That Are Mispronounced by Far Too Many People

It's really surprising how many speakers make themselves look bad by saying these words incorrectly. The second and third, particularly, are being butchered these days by what seems to be the great majority of people.

It's important to learn to pronounce these words correctly if you want to be regarded as a well-educated person.

WRONG:	RIGHT:
A*ks*	A*sk*
Ek-cet'er-a	*Et*-cet'er-a
In'*tre*-gal	In'*te*-gral (or) in-*teg*'ral
Len*th*	Len*gth*
Li'*bary*	Li'*brary*
Min'*is*-cule	Min'*us*-cule
Nuc'*u*-lar	Nu'*klee*-ar
Rec'*o*-nize	Rec'*og*-nize
Sim'*u*-lar	Sim'*i*-lar

Remember that it's icky *to say* ek *at the beginning of* etcetera. *It's just as bad to mess up* integral; *it comes from the same Latin root as* integrity. *You wouldn't say* in'*tre*-gity, *would you?*

VII. Homonyms, Homophones, and Other Confusingly Similar Words

This list of words that are most likely to be confused includes only brief and incomplete definitions because of space limitations. In many cases the words have additional meanings that are not shown. For further details I recommend that you consult a good, modern dictionary. If you don't have one handy, NOW is the time to get one!

abjure To renounce
adjure To command, as under oath

accept To receive with consent
except To exclude; to object (take exception to)

acclamation Loud expression of approval, praise, or assent
acclimation Acclimatization, especially under controlled (as laboratory) conditions

ad Advertisement
add To increase; to append

addict Person who is addicted to something, especially drugs
edict Order proclaimed by an authority

addition Something added
edition Form in which something is presented or published

adherence Act of adhering
adherents Followers

adverse Opposed; hostile
averse Having a feeling of repugnance or distaste; disinclined

advert To pay heed or attention; to refer
avert To turn away; to avoid
overt Open to view; manifest

advice (*Noun*) Information; counsel
advise (*Verb*) To offer advice

affect To have an influence on
effect To make; to bring about

affinity Close relationship
infinity Endless or unlimited space, time, etc.

affluence Abundant flow or supply
effluence Something that flows out
effluents Materials that flow out

aid Help
aide Assistant

ail To be unwell
ale Malt beverage

air Atmosphere
ere Before (*poetic*)
heir One who inherits

aisle Passageway or corridor
I'll Contraction of *I will*
isle Island (*usually poetic*)

allowed Permitted
aloud With the speaking voice

all ready Set to go
already Previously

all together Together; in concert
altogether Wholly; thoroughly

allude To refer to
elude To evade

allusion Reference
illusion Misleading image presented to the vision

allusive Containing allusions
elusive Eluding; escaping
illusive Illusory; deceptive

all ways Total number of methods
always At all times; invariably

altar (*Noun*) A usually raised platform for worship or sacrifice
alter (*Verb*) To change

amend To set right; to make emendations in
emend To correct

ant Insect
aunt Sister of one's mother or father

ante- (*Prefix*) Before
anti- (*Prefix*) Against

anyone Anybody
any one One of two or more (Any one of you would help anyone in trouble.)

anyway Nevertheless
any way No matter what means or method

appraise To evaluate or estimate
apprise To inform

arc Something arched or curved
ark Boat (Noah's); something affording protection

arrant Extreme (arrant nonsense)
errand Mission; short trip
errant Traveling; straying

assistance Help
assistants Helpers

attendance The act or fact of attending
attendants People who perform services for others; attend-
ees

aural Relating to the ear or sense of hearing
oral Spoken

bail (*Noun*) Security given for appearance of a prisoner;
(*verb*) to release under bail; to clear water from a boat
bale (*Noun*) A large bundle of goods; (*verb*) to make up into a
bale

baited Nagged or teased; set a trap
bated Restrained, reduced (bated breath)

band Something that constricts or binds
banned Prohibited

bare To uncover or reveal
bear To carry or support; endure

baron Nobleman
barren Incapable of producing offspring

beach Shore
beech Kind of tree

better Of higher quality
bettor One who bets

blew Past tense of *blow*
blue Color

boar Male hog
boor Rude or insensitive person
bore One who causes boredom

bold Fearless; impudent
bowled Past tense of *bowl*

bolder More bold
boulder Large stone

brake To arrest the motion of a mechanism
break To fracture

brews Brewed beverages
bruise Contusion; abrasion

bridal Pertaining to a bride
bridle Headgear for a horse

brilliance The quality of being brilliant
brilliants Gems (usually diamonds) with many facets

cache Hiding place; something hidden
cash Ready money

Calvary Hill near Jerusalem
cavalry Horsemen; mounted troops

cannon Artillery piece
canon Regulation; rule; dogma
canyon Deep ravine

canvas Firmly woven cloth; a sail
canvass Detailed examination; survey

capital Goods; an important city
capitol Building, usually found in a state or a national
  capital

carat Unit of weight (also spelled *karat*)
caret Wedge-shaped mark
carrot Vegetable

carousal Drunken revel
carousel Merry-go-round; airport luggage conveyor

cast Mold; a rigid dressing; actors
caste Division of society

cede To yield or grant
seed To sow

ceiling Overhead inside lining of a room
sealing Closing; fastening

censer Covered incense burner
censor To inspect conduct, morals, documents
censure To find fault with

cession Ceding; giving up; a yielding; concession
session Meeting or series of meetings of court, etc.; a period
spent continuously in an activity

cheap Inexpensive; stingy
cheep To chirp

chord Harmonious tones blended together
cord Rope; string; strands woven together (it's "vocal
cord")

cite To quote by way of example
sight (*Noun*) Something seen; (*verb*) to look at or through; to
take aim
site (*Noun*) Location; (*verb*) to locate

collaborate To work jointly with others
corroborate To get or give supporting evidence

collision Clash; impact
collusion Secret agreement or cooperation, usually for illegal purposes

complement Something that completes
compliment Expression of esteem; flattering remark

compose To form; to make up
comprise To include; to consist of (*Note:* It is incorrect to say "the apartment is comprised of three rooms.")

confidant One to whom secrets are entrusted (*male*)
confidante One to whom secrets are entrusted (*female*)
confident Full of conviction or assurance

conscience Consciousness of right or wrong
conscious Perceiving or noticing; awake

core Center
corps Group of persons associated together

dear Beloved; expensive
deer Ruminant animal

debility Feebleness; weakness
disability Something that disables or disqualifies a person

detract To take away from or lower the value
distract To divert

device Scheme; contrivance
devise To form in mind; invent; (*legal*) to give real property by will; bequeath

dew Moisture, especially in droplets
do To act
due Owing

die To cease to live
dye To color

disapprove To have or express an unfavorable opinion
disprove To refute

disburse To pay out
disperse To break up; to spread

discreet Prudent; using good judgment
discrete Individually distinct; noncontinuous

delusion False belief or opinion
disillusion Disenchantment
dissolution Act or process of dissolving

disinterested Unbiased; impartial
uninterested Not interested

dissidence Dissent; disagreement
dissidents Those who differ or disagree

dual Twofold
duel Combat between two persons

emigrant One who leaves one's country
immigrant One who comes to a country to take up residence

eminent Prominent; outstanding
immanent Inherent; existing in consciousness of the mind
imminent About to happen

ensure To make certain; to insure
insure To give, take, or procure insurance on; to take necessary measures
assure To give confidence to

everyone Everybody
every one Each one

exalt To raise high; to glorify
exult To rejoice

exceptionable Objectionable
exceptional Rare; better than average

exercise To use; to exert oneself physically or mentally
exorcise To expel, as an evil spirit

expand To increase; to enlarge
expend To spend; to consume

explicit Free from ambiguity
implicit Implied

explode To burst (out) violently
implode To burst inward

facility Quality of being easy; an aid, equipment, structure, and so forth that makes it easy to do something
faculty Any of the powers of body or mind; teaching and administrative staff of a school

fair Impartial
fare Price charged to transport a person

farther At or to a greater distance or more advanced point
further In addition; moreover

fay Fairy; elf
fey Crazy; touched

faze To disconcert
phase To adjust so as to synchronize

feat Notable act or achievement
feet Plural of *foot*

final At the end; coming last
finale The final section of a musical composition, event, etc.

find To come upon, often accidentally
fined Subjected to a penalty

fir Evergreen tree
fur Pelt; coat

flair Natural aptitude
flare Unsteady, glaring light

flammable Inflammable
inflammable Able to be set on fire

flaunt To display in a gaudy manner
flout To scorn; to mock (He flouts convention.)

floe Large mass of floating ice
flow Uninterrupted movement

forbear To abstain; to forgo
forebear Ancestor

foreword Preface
forward Situated in advance
froward Habitually disposed to disobedience

formally Ceremoniously; conventionally
formerly Previously

forth Onward; forward
fourth Number four in series

fortuitous Happening by chance; accidental
fortunate Lucky

foul Offensive
fowl Bird, especially domestic cock or hen

gaff Sharp hook for spearing fish
gaffe Social blunder

gait Manner of walking
gate Opening in a wall or fence

gibe To utter taunting words
jibe To be in accord; (*nautical*) to shift suddenly

gorilla Ape
guerrilla One who engages in irregular warfare

gourmand Lover of food; a glutton
gourmet Connoisseur of good food and drink

graffiti Plural of *graffito*
graffito Words or drawing scratched or scribbled on a wall

hail To welcome
hale Healthy

hall Large room for assembly
haul To pull with force

halve To divide in half
have To be in possession of

hangar Shelter for an airplane
hanger One who hangs; loop or device for hanging

hay Dried grass
hey Expression of surprise or exultation

holey Containing holes
holy Sacred
wholly Completely; entirely

homogeneous Of the same or a similar kind of nature
homogenous Relating to mating like with like

hours Sixty-minute periods
ours Yours and mine (no apostrophe!)

human Of or relating to a person
humane Marked by compassion

hyper- (*Prefix*) Above or beyond (hypertension: high blood pressure)
hypo- (*Prefix*) Less than or below normal

hypercritical Excessively critical
hypocritical Characterized by hypocrisy

idle Not occupied; unemployed
idol Symbol of worship; false god
idyll Narrative poem; romantic interlude

immoral Not moral
immortal Exempt from death or oblivion

immunity State of being protected from a disease
impunity Exemption or freedom from punishment or harm

inane Silly; lacking sense
insane Not sane; mad

incidence Rate of occurrence or influence
incidents Occurrences; happenings

incredible Hard to believe; unbelievable
incredulous Skeptical; unbelieving, showing disbelief

independence Freedom
independents People not subjected to control by others

indeterminable Impossible to discover or decide
indeterminate Not fixed in extent or character; vague

indiscreet Imprudent
indiscrete Not separated into parts

inequity Injustice; unfairness
iniquity Wickedness

infect To contaminate
infest To overrun in large numbers
inject To introduce a new element into

its Possessive pronoun (*Note:* It never takes an apostrophe!)
it's Contraction of *it is*

jam Crush; difficult spot; jelly
jamb Side of a door or window

jealous Envious
zealous Ardent

jiggle To rock or jerk lightly
joggle To shake slightly; to move by light jerks
juggle To toss and catch a number of objects skillfully

judicial Pertaining to courts of law
judicious Wise; discreet
juridical Of or relating to the administration of justice

knave Rogue
nave Main part of church interior

knead To press with the hands (as dough); to mold
kneed Struck with the knee
need To want; to lack

knew Past tense of *know*
new Recent; novel

knight Medieval gentleman-soldier
night Opposite of day

knit To link or cause to grow together
nit Louse or its egg

knot Tying; lump or knob
naught Nothing; zero
not Negative

lade To load
laid Past tense of *lay* (He laid it down.)
[layed] No such word!

leach To subject to the action of percolating liquid (leaching field)
leech Sucking worm

lead (*Noun*) Metallic element
led (*Verb*) Conducted

levee Embankment
levy Assessment

lean Lacking in fat
lien Legal right to a debtor's property

legislator One who legislates
legislature Body of persons having power to make laws

lends Makes a loan
lens Optical glass; part of eye (plural: *lenses*)

lessen To shrink or decrease
lesson Something learned or studied

lesser Of less size, quality, or significance
lessor One who conveys property by lease

lets Allows
let's Contraction of *let us*

liable Responsible; subject to something possible or likely
libel To defame, usually in writing

lichen Type of funguslike plant
liken To compare

lie Falsehood
lye Caustic substance

loath Unwilling; reluctant
loathe To detest

macr-, macro- (*Prefix*) Long; large
micr-, micro- (*Prefix*) Small; minute

macrocosm The great world; the universe
microcosm World in miniature

made Manufactured
maid Young girl; servant

magnate Person of power or influence
magnet Something that attracts

magnificent Grand; sumptuous
munificent Lavish; liberal

main Principal
Maine New England state
mane Long hair growing around the neck

mall Area set aside as for shopping
maul To beat; to handle roughly

maniac Lunatic; madman
manic Afflicted with or pertaining to a mania

manner Way of acting (to the manner born)
manor Mansion

mantel Shelf above a fireplace
mantle Cloak

marital Of or relating to marriage
martial Warlike

marshal Officer in charge of prisoners; leader of parade
Marshall Common surname

massif Principal mountain mass
massive Bulky; weighty; heavy

material Matter; goods
matériel Equipment and supplies used by an organization

mean A middle point between extremes
mien Bearing; demeanor

medal Piece of metal, usually with a stamped design, given
    as an award
meddle To interfere
metal Any of various fusible, ductile, lustrous substances
mettle Quality of temperament or disposition; courage

miner One who works in a mine
minor One who has not attained majority

minks Certain fur-bearing animals; furs
minx Pert girl

misogamy Hatred of marriage
misogyny Hatred of women

missed Failed to hit or reach
mist Fine rain; a film

moan Low sound of pain; a lament
mown Past tense of *mow*

mode Manner; style
mowed Alternate past tense of *mow*

moot Open to question; debatable; made abstract or purely academic
mute Characterized by absence of speech or sound

moral Significance or lesson to be drawn from a story
morale Individual's mental and emotional condition

morality Moral conduct; virtue
mortality Quality or state of being mortal (mortality table: actuarial table)

morning Forenoon
mourning The act of sorrowing

motif Dominant idea or theme (as in a work of art)
motive Something (as a need or desire) that causes a person to act

mucous (*Adjective*) Secreting or containing mucus
mucus (*Noun*) Viscid bodily secretion

muscat Grape
musket Heavy shoulder gun

nauseated Affected with nausea
nauseous Causing nausea

nay A negative reply or vote
né or **née** Born with the name of
neigh The cry of a horse

neither Not either
nether Situated down or below

neuter Neither masculine nor feminine (of a noun)
neutral Not aligned with any side

none Not any; nothing
nun Female member of a religious order

oar Long pole for propelling a boat
o'er Over (*poetic*)
or Conjunction suggesting an alternative
ore Mineral containing valuable metal

obsequies Funeral rites; a funeral
obsequious Excessively or sickeningly respectful

ode Lyric poem
owed Obligated to

odious Hateful; detestable
odorous Smelly

official Of an office or position of authority; authenticated; authorized
officious Asserting one's authority; bossy

omnipotent Having unlimited power or very great power
omniscient Knowing everything

ordinance Authoritative decree or direction
ordnance Military supplies, weapons, ammunition, etc.

organism A living being; an individual animal or plant
orgasm Sexual climax

pail Bucket
pale Deficient in color

pain Discomfort
pane Framed sheet of glass

pair Twosome
pare To trim; to peel
pear Fruit

palate Roof of the mouth
palette Thin board on which a painter mixes pigments
pallet Small temporary bed; portable platform

palpate To examine by touch
palpitate To beat rapidly; to throb

parlay To increase or otherwise transform into something
of much greater value
parley To confer; to discuss terms with an enemy

passed Moved; departed; overtook
past Relating to an earlier period

peal To ring (as a bell)
peel To strip off an outer layer

pedal (*Noun*) Foot lever; (*verb*) to ride a bicycle
peddle To sell or offer to sell from place to place
petal Portion of a flower

pediatrist Specialist in children's diseases
podiatrist One who takes care of feet

peer One who is of equal standing with another
pier Supporting structure, as for adjacent ends of two
bridge spans

penal Pertaining to punishment
penile Relating to or affecting the penis

penance Act showing repentance
pennants Flags; banners

pendant Something suspended, as an ornament
pendent Supported from above; suspended

penitence Feeling of remorse for wrongdoing
penitents Persons who show remorse for wrongdoing

peremptory Admitting of no contradiction (peremptory challenge)
pre-emptory Pertaining to prior rights

persecute To harass
prosecute To follow to the end; to institute and carry on legal proceedings

personal Relating to a person; private
personnel Makeup of an office force

perspective Outlook; vista; view
prospective Likely to happen; expected

perverse Obstinate; intractable
perverted Turned from its proper course or use

physic A medicine, especially a purgative
physique Bodily makeup
psychic Of or relating to the soul, spirit, or mind

picaresque Of or relating to rogues or rascals
picturesque Resembling a picture; vivid; graphic

picture A portrait
pitcher Jug for holding liquids

plaintiff One who commences legal action
plaintive Melancholy

poor Indigent
pore To gaze at intently
pour To cause to flow in a stream

portent Omen
potent Powerful; strong

precede To surpass in rank or importance; to be, go, or come ahead
proceed To continue; to go in an orderly way; to advance

precedence Fact of preceding in time; priority (Sometimes pronounced with long "e" in second syllable.)
precedents (*Legal*) Adjudged cases or decisions considered as authority for later similar case

preceding Going before in time or place
proceeding Legal action (often used in plural); transaction

precipitate Headlong
precipitous Steep

premise Something taken for granted
premises Tract of land with buildings thereon; house or other building

prescribe To lay down as a guide, direction, or rule of action; to order the use of as a remedy
proscribe To condemn or forbid as harmful; prohibit. (*Note:* These two words have almost exactly opposite meanings.)

presence The fact or condition of being present
presents Gifts

presentiment Foreboding
presentment Act of presenting

presumptive Giving grounds for presumption
presumptuous Behaving with impudent boldness

preview Advance showing
purview Scope, intention, or range, especially of a law

primer (Long "i") Substance used to prepare a surface for painting; detonator for explosives
primer (Short "i") Elementary textbook
primmer More prim

principal Person who has controlling authority; leading performer
principle Rule or code of conduct

profit Gain
prophet One who predicts the future

prophecy Prediction
prophesy To foretell

qualify To modify; to exhibit a required degree of ability to
    perform in some capacity
quantify To determine the quantity of

qualitative Of, relating to, or involving quality or kind
quantitative Of, relating to, or expressible in terms of quan-
    tity

quarts Units of capacity
quartz Mineral

quash To annul; to reject (by legal authority) as not valid
squash To crush; to squeeze

quiet Tranquility
quit To cease
quite Wholly; to a considerable extent; rather

rain To fall as water; to pour down
rein To check or stop
reign To rule

rack To cause to suffer torture; to stretch violently
wrack To ruin utterly; to destroy (You rack your brains;
    wracking would destroy them.)

raise To elevate; to build
rays Beams of light
raze To destroy to the ground

rap A sharp blow or knock
wrap An outer garment or covering (gift wrap)

rapped Tapped or knocked
rapt Enraptured; absorbed
wrapped Enveloped

rational Having reason or understanding
rationale Underlying reason; basis

read To peruse
reed Tall grass

real Actual; genuine
reel Revolving device on which something flexible is wound

realign To align again or regroup
reline To line again

reck To reckon
wreck To ruin or damage

remuneration Payment for services rendered
[renumeration] No such word!

residence Domicile
residency Place of residence, usually official; period of advanced training in a medical specialty
residents Those who reside in a place

rest To repose
wrest To gain by force or violence

resume To get, take, or occupy again
résumé Summary

retch To try to vomit
wretch Miserable and unhappy person; a vile person

reverend Worthy of reverence; (with "the") a member of the clergy
reverent Expressing reverence; worshipful

review Inspection, especially military; survey; critical examination

revue Theatrical production usually consisting of short skits, dances, etc.

right Entitlement; privilege

rite Ceremony

wright Workman (*Note:* Used now mostly in compounds: millwright, playwright.)

write To form characters on a surface as with a pen

ring To sound (as a bell); to reverberate; to encircle

wring To squeeze or twist, especially so as to make dry

saccharin Sugar substitute

saccharine Intensely and unpleasantly sweet

scene Subdivision of a play

seen Form of verb *to see*

scull An oar used at the stern of a boat; a racing shell

skull The framework of the head

sculptor Artist who produces a sculpture

sculpture A three-dimensional work of art

sea Body of water

see To perceive by the eye

seam The joining of two pieces

seem To appear (to be)

seasonable Suitable for the season; timely

seasonal Of a season or seasons

secretively Carried out with secrecy

secretly Kept from knowledge or view

sensual Physical; gratifying to the body
sensuous Affecting or appealing to the senses, especially by beauty or delicacy

serge Durable twilled fabric
surge Swelling, rolling, or sweeping forward, like waves of the ocean

sew To unite or fasten by stitches
so Thus
sow To plant seed, especially by scattering

shear To cut (as hair or wool)
sheer To deviate from a course; swerve

sleight Stratagem; dexterity (sleight of hand)
slight Slim; frail; meager

sniffle To sniff slightly or repeatedly
snivel To whine

soar To fly aloft or about; to rise to heights; to glide
sore Painful

sole Undersurface of foot or footwear
soul Spirit

solid Keeping its shape; firm; not liquid or gas
stolid Not feeling or showing emotion

stalactite Hanging calcium deposit
stalagmite Upright calcium deposit

stanch To restrain the flow (as of blood)
staunch Firm in attitude, opinion, or loyalty

stationary Immobile; fixed
stationery Writing paper

stile Series of steps for passing over a fence or wall
style Fashion

stimulant Agent (as a drug) that produces a temporary increase in activity
stimulus Something that rouses or incites to activity

straight Direct; uninterrupted; upright
strait (*Adjective*) Narrow, constricted; (*noun*) an isthmus (Strait of Gibraltar, straightjacket, straitlaced—but straightedge)

summary (*Adjective*) Quickly executed
summery Of, resembling, or fit for summer

systematic Relating to or consisting of a system
systemic Relating to or common to a system; affecting the body generally

tail Rear appendage
tale Story

team To yoke or join in a team
teem To abound; to become filled to overflowing

tenant Lessee; occupant
tenet Principle, belief, or doctrine held to be true

terminable Able to be terminated
terminal At the end

tern Type of sea gull
turn Rotation

their Possessive pronoun
there In that place
they're Contraction of *they are*

theirs Possessive pronoun (*Note:* Never takes an apostrophe!)
there's Contraction of *there is* or *there has*

thorough Painstaking
through Extending from one surface to another; finished

thrash To beat soundly with a stick or whip
thresh To beat out or separate (grain) from husks

throes Pangs; spasms (death throes; in the throes of . . .)
throws Tosses

throne Chair of state for a king
thrown Tossed

tic Muscular twitching, especially of the face
tick Light, rhythmic tap or beat; bloodsucking arachnid

tide Alternate rising and falling of ocean
tied Past tense of *tie*

timber Growing trees or their wood
timbre Quality given to a sound by its overtones

to Toward
too Also
two Number

toad Tailless, leaping amphibian
toed Having toes
towed Past tense of *tow*

toe To touch, reach, or drive with the foot (toe the mark)
tow To draw or pull along behind

tort Wrongful act
torte Kind of rich, round layer cake

tortuous Winding; circuitous; tricky or crooked
torturous Causing torture; cruelly painful

turbid Obscure; muddy
turgid Swollen; pompous

undo Unfasten; nullify
undue Exceeding or violating propriety or fitness

[unequivocably] No such word!
unequivocally Leaving no doubt; unambiguous

unexceptionable Beyond reproach
unexceptional Commonplace

unreal Lacking in reality
unreel To unwind from a reel

unstated Unsaid
understated Stated in restrained terms

unwanted Not wanted
unwonted Rare; unusual

urban Of, relating to, or constituting a city
urbane Suave; sophisticated

vain Conceited
vane Device showing wind direction
vein Narrow channel; lode; blood vessel

valance Short curtain
valence Capacity of an atom to combine with another or
others

variance Dispute; deviation
variants Persons or things exhibiting usually slight differ-
ences

vary To change; to deviate
very Exceedingly

veracious Truthful
voracious Ravenously hungry

vertex Highest point of something
vortex Whirling mass of fluid; something resembling a whirlpool

vice Moral fault or failing
vise Tool with tight-holding jaws

visible Able to be seen or noticed
visual Of or used in seeing; received through sight

wail Mournful cry
wale Rib in fabric; ridge
whale Sea mammal

waist The narrowed part of the body between thorax and hips
waste Rejected material; garbage

wait Delay
weight Heaviness

waive To relinquish voluntarily
wave To motion with the hand

waiver Voluntary relinquishment of a right or privilege
waver To vacillate

walk Stroll; sidewalk
wok Cooking utensil

want Lack
wont Custom
won't Contraction of *will not*

ward To deflect (usually used with *off*)
warred Made war on

ware Goods
wear To bear or have on the person
where At, in, or to what place

warrantee Person to whom a warranty is made (*Note:* Never is properly used as a verb.)
warranty A guarantee (*Note:* This is a noun only; the verb is *warrant*.)

way Thoroughfare
weigh To ascertain the heaviness of
whey Thin part of milk

weak Lacking strength
week Seven days

weather State of atmosphere as to heat, cold, and so forth
whether If it be the case that

whither To which place
wither To dry up

whose Of or relating to whom or which, especially as possessor or possessors
who's Contraction of *who is* or *who has*

y'all You-all
yawl Kind of sailboat
yowl Long, loud, mournful wail or howl

yoke Wooden frame for joining together draft animals
yolk Yellow of an egg

yore Time long past
your Personal pronoun

VIII. Errors in the Test Story

The text on pages 1 through 3 contains 88 goofs, listed below in order of their appearance, with the corrections in parentheses:

nations (*nation's*)
capital (*capitol*)
sight (*site*)
imminent (*eminent*)
core (*corps*)
Its' (*It's*)
myself (*me*)
discretely (*discreetly*)
navel (*naval*)
aid (*aide*)
surge (*serge*)
less (*fewer*)
like (*as if* or *as though*)
acclimation (*acclamation*)
vary (*very*)
whether (*weather*)
seam (*seem*)
phase (*faze*)
reign (*rein*)
between . . . to
  (*between . . . and*)
  (or *from . . . to*)
rapped (*rapt*)
stationery (*stationary*)
like (*as if* or *as though*)

vice (*vise*)
their (*there*)
incidence (*incidents*)
never (*ever*)
pail (*pale*)
use (*used*)
worse (*worst*)
scene (*seen*)
I (*me*)
its (*it's*)
anymore (*nowadays* or
  lately)
try and (*try to*)
lay (*lie*)
were'nt (*weren't*)
principals (*principles*)
metal (*mettle*)
peddling (*pedaling*)
exorcise (*exercise*)
vain (*vein*)
tail (*tale*)
better (*bettor*)
shear (*sheer*)
miner (*minor*)
pealing (*peeling*)
advise (*advice*)

83

council (*counsel*)
gamboler (*gambler*)
waved (*waived*)
through (*threw*)
ringing (*wringing*)
sealing (*ceiling*)
bale (*bail*)
meeted (*meted*)
leveed (*levied*)
good (*well*)
lessen (*lesson*)
prophet (*profit*)
sew (*sow*)
weather (*whether*)
nation's (*nations*)
reek (*wreak*)
saver (*savor*)
piece (*peace*)
teaming (*teeming*)
disburse (*disperse*)

pare (*pair*)
who's (*whose*)
bridle (*bridal*)
further (*farther*)
pouring (*poring*)
to who (*to whom*)
Like (*As*)
its (*it's*)
alot (*a lot*)
not (*knot*)
undue (*undo*)
loose (*lose*)
site (*sight*)
strait (*straight*)
there (*their*)
allusion (*illusion*)
ware (*wear*)
bullion (*bouillon*)
like (*as if* or *as though*)
sleight (*slight*)

Mark Twain said it best:
"The difference between the right word
and the *almost* right word is the difference
between lightning and the lightning bug."

GOOF-PROOF YOUR FRIENDS!

Yes! I know someone who can benefit from the advice in your books. Please send a copy(ies) of *The Goof-Proofer* to the address below. Return this coupon to: Macmillan Publishing Company, Special Sales Department, 866 Third Avenue, New York, NY 10022.

Line Sequence	ISBN	Title	Price	Quantity
1	002040610x	*The Goof-Proofer*	$3.95	___

Please add postage and handling costs—$1.00 for the first book and 50¢ for each additional book ___

Sales tax—if applicable ___

TOTAL ═══

	Lines	Units

___ Enclosed is my check/money order payable to Macmillan Publishing Company.

___ Bill my ___ MasterCard ___ Visa Card # ___ Control No. [   ] Ord. Type [REG]

For charge orders only:

Expiration date ___ Signature ___

Charge orders valid only with signature

Ship to:

Bill to:

_____

_____ Zip Code ___

_____

_____ Zip Code ___

For information regarding bulk purchases, please write to Special Sales Director at the above address. Publisher's prices are subject to change without notice. Allow 3 weeks for delivery.   FC #890